HOPI
KACHINAS

Soyok wuhti

HOPI KACHINAS

by Edward A. Kennard

illustrations by Edwin Earle

KIVA
PUBLISHING, INC.

Library of Congress Cataloging-in-Publication Data

Kennard, Edward A. (Edward Allan), 1907-
    Hopi kachinas / by Edward A. Kennard ; illustrations by Edwin Earle.
        p. cm.
Originally published: New York: J.J. Augustin, c1938.
Includes bibliographical references.
    ISBN 1-885772-28-9 (pbk.)
1. Kachinas. 2. Hopi Indians–Religion. I. Earle, Edwin, 1904-II.
Title.
    E99.H7 K45 2002
    299'.7845–dc21

                            2002008581

Text and cover Design by Rudy Ramos

Printed in USA by ALI Graphic Services Inc.

9 8 7 6 5 4 3 2 1

Kiva Publishing
21731 E. Buckskin Drive, Walnut, CA 91789

Publisher's Foreword

*H*OPI *KACHINAS,* first published in 1938 by J.J. Augustin, soon became a classic in the field of Indian religious expression. Long recognized by scholars, especially anthropologists and ethnologists, this book was the first non-academic publication to discuss the traditional kachina ceremonial cycle with references only to color plates representing the kachina dancers. Illustrator Edwin Earle and author Edward A. Kennard were both privileged to personally observe the ceremonies they depicted.

In 1971, the Museum of the American Indian, Heye Foundation, published a revised second edition. In his Publisher's Foreword, museum director Frederick J. Dockstader indicated that this volume had been out of print for some time, available only as a rare edition. The revised edition added several titles to the selected bibliography, including only three published after 1938.

The second edition has now been out of print for many years. In the meantime, many new kachina titles have emerged, most of them dwelling on kachina dolls rather than the religious ceremonialism behind them. In recent years, numerous Hopi carvers have produced kachina dolls that range from traditional depictions to items for the tourist trade. The general public is familiar with kachinas primarily through these representations.

Why publish a new print edition of this book in the twenty-first century, when we are on the threshold of a digital technology revolution that will bring virtually any graphic or reading material to any reader with access to a computer? Fundamentally, the value of a book such as *Hopi Kachinas* is in its relationship to traditions, of both Hopi religion and the printed book.

The Hopi religious ceremonies witnessed by Dr. Kennard in the 1930's are rarely seen today in the same form. As Kennard suggests, certain kachinas do not appear regularly, and indeed their absence in today's ceremonies may not be a random occurrence, but rather a result of a decline in the passing down of traditional knowledge. Thus, the text and illustrations in this book represent a moment in time, based on direct observations by both author and illustrator. In today's world, the opportunity to observe Hopi ceremonies is far more restricted than it was in the early twentieth century, when numerous observers, many of them anthropologists, were welcomed as students of Hopi life.

Preface to the First Edition

I AM INDEBTED to the Laboratory of Anthropology at Santa Fe, the Council for Research in the Social Sciences, Columbia University, and the Federal Writers' Project for the opportunity to work among the Hopi between 1932 and the present time, and hereby express my gratitude to all of these institutions. Although my part in this book is a by-product of work on Hopi language and culture, it would not have been possible without the assistance granted by the institutions named above.

I also wish to acknowledge my appreciation of the assistance rendered by many Hopis at Oraibi, who prefer to remain anonymous for obvious reasons.

EDWARD A. KENNARD
Toreva, Arizona
August 1938

Table of Contents

List of Illustrations

Introduction

THE KACHINAS REPRESENTED in this volume were all sketched by the artist during his residence at Oraibi in 1932 and 1934-5. Once the largest of the Hopi villages, Oraibi is no longer representative of their ceremonial life. However, from the original parental community three others have grown—Hotevilla, Pakavi, and Kiquchmovi, and in the first the complete cycle of ceremonies is still flourishing. In Pakavi only a few of the rites of old Oraibi are still active, but the most prominent are the Kachina dances. Even in Kiquchmovi, the settlement at the foot of the mesa composed largely of those who have abandoned their ancient customs, life still seems dreary without the gaiety and color brought by the masked dancers. So, here too, the gods still make their appearance.

Edwin Earle observed performances at all of these places, as well as at Walpi and the Middle Mesa villages. However, all of his sketches were reviewed by Hopis from Oraibi and Hotevilla, and the text will be confined to the organization and performances at old Oraibi. For this reason, the Kachina cult will be described as it was in Oraibi before 1907, the year of the first split in the village. There is no intention of implying that Kachina dancing is a thing of the past in any of the Hopi villages. The truth is quite the opposite. It is flourishing today both as a religious system and as an art form. Even at Oraibi the masked gods played their accustomed role during Mr. Earle's stay, although there have been no dances during the past two years. However, in order to make the present account both accurate and complete, it is carried back to a time when none of the disruptions of Oraibi's recent history had yet occurred.

In selecting these particular figures from the artist's collection of more than one hundred Kachinas, several factors have been taken into consideration. First, most of the Chief Kachinas, the figures which always appear at specific times during the year, have been included because it is felt that this is an honest reflection of Hopi values. Second, all of the most popular dancing Kachinas—those most frequently presented when there is practically an unlimited choice—have been selected. Third, the others have been chosen to illustrate the extent of variation in this particular art.

The Role of Kachinas in Hopi Life

THE HOPI INDIANS live in nine villages built upon three high rocky mesas in north-eastern Arizona. Each village is laid out around one or more open plazas which provide the theater for the performance of the annual cycle of dramatic dances and ceremonies. They are the predominant interest of the people, the focal point of most of their thought and energy, and the most characteristic expression of their genius.

Although the Snake Dance, occurring in the last days of August, has attracted the most attention and draws great throngs of visitors from the outside world, no such emphasis is placed upon it by the Hopi. For them it is but one of many rites, each of which has its fixed place in the calendar, and its eight days of esoteric activity are as secret to the uninitiated Hopi as they are to the casual visitor. The Kachina cult, however, is distinguished from the others in that every man, woman, and child is initiated into it, and every man takes an active part in its dances throughout his life. Furthermore, fully half the year is devoted to the various ceremonies which are part of the cult and the ideas associated with it are constantly reflected in daily life and folklore. The dolls that the girls play with are carved from wood painted, and feathered in the same way as the Kachinas. The bows and arrows of the boys are given to them by the Kachinas. The designs of the women's baskets are frequently taken from the masks of Kachinas, and the songs most frequently sung are those of the Kachinas.

The term Kachina in Hopi applies to a number of distinct things which are all associated in the Hopi mind. It refers to the masked and painted impersonation, to the spiritual being impersonated, to the clouds, and to the dead. The Kachinas are thought to live in the San Francisco Mountains, where they remain during half of the year when there are no masked dances in the village. During the other half of the year, they come to the village to dance, sing, bring presents for the children, and above all to bring rain. When they dance, they summon their "cloud fathers," another form in which the Kachinas appear. It is generally believed that the spirits of the dead go to the west where they become Kachinas and return to the village as clouds. When a man dies, a white cotton batting is placed over his face, referred to as his cloud mask.

Hopi interests, however, are centered much more upon the actual appearance and performance of the Kachinas in the village than on the ideological background. While any Hopi can describe in detail the costume, songs, and dance steps of a great number of Kachinas, he remains comfortably vague on the subject of their relations to the forces of the universe, the nature of their power, and the fate of the soul after death. Frequently, members of other cult groups hold beliefs at variance with those of the Kachina cult. All ceremonies are for rain, and the correct performance of numerous ritual acts brings the desired result. The order and systematization of their life is found in the arrangement of a number of distinct religious societies, each performing at a fixed time during the year, each involving many individuals performing different functions in different groups, all following prescribed rituals in detail, and all coordinated to make up the religious life of the people. But this feeling for organization so characteristic of their life is not reflected in their thought. There is no tendency to develop a unified conception of the universe, to identify specific deities of their mythology with natural forces, nor to arrange them in a hierarchical system.

Apart from their supernatural power and the blessings they bestow with the rain, the Kachinas are thought of as friends, and they are endowed with many human characteristics. They dance and sing in their kivas, plant and cultivate their corn, their wives grind it into meal, they war against their enemies, and steal one another's wives. Each has a personality in a very limited sense. Each is distinguished not only by the painting and decoration of his mask and body, but also by his songs, his dance step, his call, and his bearing. One moves across the plaza with long swaggering steps, another dances lightly from place to place, while a third moves with stately dignity. Some are silly and act as clowns to amuse the spectators, and others are mean to inspire fear in the hearts of the uninitiated.

Back of the appearance of the Kachinas in procession and dance lies a complex organization, involving not only this particular type of ceremony, but many others as well. In order to understand the role they play in the life of the Hopi, it is necessary to see their religious activities as a whole.

Each year there is a succession of ceremonies, and their order and occurrence is determined by a calendar based on a combination of solar and lunar observations. In order to clarify the arrangement of this series, it can be outlined in terms of our named months as follows:

December	Winter Solstice
February	Powamu
July	Niman
August	Snake or Flute
September	Marau
October	Oaqöl
November	Wuwuchim

The new year begins with the Winter Solstice rites, during the course of which everything is prepared for the coming year. It is followed in February by the Powamu, one of the two major ceremonies connected with the Kachina cult. In mid-July, the Niman Kachina celebration occurs, marking the departure of the masked gods from Oraibi. This is usually referred to as the Home Dance because the Kachinas are thought to go to their home in the San Francisco Mountains, where they remain for the next half year. The Snake Dance alternates annually with the Flute Ceremony at the end of August. Each of these rites involves the simultaneous performance of two distinct groups, but in both instances their activities are complementary. The Snake rites are performed by the collaboration of the Snake and the Antelope Societies. In alternate years, two distinct Flute Societies collaborate. The Marau and the Oaqöl are both women's societies and perform in September and October respectively. The Wuwuchim is one of the most complicated of all Hopi rites. It is named from one of four societies which perform simultaneously in November and includes all the adult men, since every man must be initiated into one of these four groups.

Every year seven major ceremonies take place, and all possess certain features in common. Each is conducted by one or more chiefs whose offices are hereditary. Each begins with an announcement at sunrise, has eight days of secret rites, and is concluded with a public dance on the ninth day. Each has as its primary aim the production of rain, fertility, and growth. Each imposes purification taboos upon its members. In addition, all ceremonies use the following specific techniques: preparation and offering of prayer sticks, building an altar of sacred objects, smoking, sprinkling medicine, prayer, song, and dance.

At the head of the organization of Oraibi is the Chief of Houses (Village Chief) who is also the leader of the Winter Solstice observances. Assisting him is the Crier, whose only function is to announce from the housetop the date for each ceremony, determined by the observation of the place where the sun sets on the horizon. All the other officers are the leaders of specific religious societies. For the Kachina cult there are two officers, Powamu Chief and Kachina Chief, leaders of the Powamu and the Niman ceremonies respectively. They, like all Hopi chiefs, are the possessors of a very sacred object called a tiponi, kept in the back room of their houses. Only when his society is in session does the leader move the tiponi to the kiva, where it occupies a prominent place on the altar.

From the point of view of Kachina celebrations, the ceremonial calendar can be divided into two halves. Although two Kachinas appear in connection with the Winter Solstice, the season really begins on the final day of those rites. At that time a group of Qöqölo Kachinas (PLATE III) appear and at the entrance to each kiva make a line with cornmeal on the north, west, south, and east sides in order. This symbolizes the opening of the kivas so that the Kachinas can come out. From that time until the final day of the Home Dance in July, the Kachinas are thought to be in and around Oraibi. They stay at their homes nearby, at shrines and springs bearing names associated with them. The number of these sacred places is legion, and they are constantly referred to in song and prayer. They are also the places where offerings of prayer sticks and sacred meal are made for the Kachinas. From these places they come often to Oraibi to bring the rain, bless the village, bestow their gifts, and gladden the hearts of the people with songs and dances. They are the paramount interest of the Hopi until their departure in July.

The Kachina performances differ from all other ceremonies in several respects. They are never announced from the housetop by the Crier, for the fiction must be maintained that the gods come to visit the people of their own will. Were they announced, it would be impossible to keep the secret of impersonation from the children. Furthermore, they are not limited to the two major rites mentioned, but come to dance, to punish the children, and to race for prizes on many occasions during the half year that they are in and around the village. They are the only Hopi ceremonies that use masks. Supernatural beings are impersonated in other rites, but the mask distinguishes the impersonation of Kachinas from all others.

There are two kinds of Kachinas which are quite distinct. Most of them are chosen according to the desires of the people, and masks are painted and redecorated for each appearance. However, there is another type called Chief Kachinas, whose masks are permanent and are carefully kept in the back rooms of houses. They only appear at specified times during the year. The right to have these masks and to wear them is hereditary like the possession of a tiponi, and like the tiponi the mask is a sacred object and great power is attributed to it. Some of them appear in the Winter Solstice ceremony and the Poamu every year as Soyal Kachina (PLATE I), Mastop Kachina (PLATE II), Eototo (PLATE IV), and Aholi (PLATE V). Others are seen only during the years when the children are initiated into the Kachina cult as Hu' Kachina (PLATE VII). Chief Kachinas never dance in groups. They are in general more aloof and awe-inspiring than the dancers, and their masks are not so elaborate. In a sense they occupy positions in the Kachina world analogous to the positions held by the Hopi Chiefs in Oraibi, but only one corresponds to any Hopi office; Eototo is regarded as the Village Chief.

Old Oraibi had twelve kivas (underground ceremonial rooms). When a child reached the age of seven to ten years, the parents selected a man to act as a sponsor during the initiation. In this way the child became a member of his sponsor's kiva, and participated in the dances presented by that group. Everyone is initiated, and learns the secret of the use of masks, but only the boys take an active part after their induction into the cult. The Kachina cult has two divisions—Powamu and Kachina—and the child belongs to the same division as his sponsor. Only those who are members of the Powamu division can act as "father" to the Kachinas. When there is a dance, they lead in the line, sprinkle the dancers with cornmeal, and answer the words of their songs.

There are two series of Kachina dances performed annually. In January, after the end of the Winter Solstice ceremony, each of the kivas prepares a series of masked dancers. They appear only in the kivas at night, but one group appears from each kiva so that as many as twelve different kinds of Kachinas are seen in the course of a single night. During the winter months there may be three or four night dances of this type. In April, May, and June the Kachinas come to dance in the plaza. Generally, there is only one kind on each dance day, but they dance all day long and the number of performers is much greater. There are usually three or four dances of this type, culminating in the Home Dance. These are the occasions when the clowns come out to amuse the spectators, when throngs of visitors from other villages come to see the dance, and the day is devoted to feasting in a holiday spirit.

Frequently, the kivas prepare racing Kachinas. They generally enter one end of the plaza late in the afternoon, and offer prizes of fruit, bread, and various kinds of Hopi food to anyone who can beat them to the opposite end. If a boy wins, he gets the prize. Should he lose, his penalty varies with the Kachina who beats him. One blackens his face, another cuts his hair with shears he carries, a third rips off his shirt. Others escort the defeated to women who douse him with cold water. They race until no one challenges them. A few days later another group of racers from a different kiva will come out and the races are repeated. Thus, during the course of the season every kiva is represented in this way as well as in the night dances.

Materials for Kachina Impersonation

THE ACTUAL NUMBER of kachinas known to the Hopi is beyond computation. About 190 were drawn for J. W. Fewkes by the Hopis at Walpi more than forty years ago and published in his study of "Hopi Katcinas." New ones are constantly being created, and several have come into existence since his study was made. Navan Kachina (PLATE XXIV) is regarded as a new Kachina, and the use of a velvet shirt and silk ribbons as part of the costume support this theory. Some old ones under go modification, as the Qöqölo Kachina (PLATE III) which nowadays always wears old clothes of white manufacture, whereas it formerly had a costume of buckskin. However, most of them have remained remarkably consistent, as a comparison of Angakchina (PLATE XVI) with the one in Fewkes' collection reveals no apparent differences. Many Kachinas are known because of the tales told about them and are hardly ever represented in dances. Others may be impersonated only once in ten years. It is likely that several hundred are known and have appeared within the lifetime of any older man.

Another factor influencing the variety presented is popular taste. Certain Kachinas seem to enjoy sustained popularity and are presented every year because the people like them. Tasap Kachina (PLATES XII and XIII) and Apgakchina (PLATE XVI) have been danced every year for the past six years and are among those most frequently described by the early writers. On the other hand, several Kachinas often mentioned in earlier days are rarely seen today.

Every Kachina is named, but the significance of the names varies, and they have been arrived at in many ways. Many bear names that are not descriptive nor subject to translation, as Eototo, Aholi, Chaveyo, and Mastop. Others are named for some animal or Bird— Bear, Snake, Squirrel, Deer, Hawk, Bluebird, and Owl. The names of a third group are derived from their calls, one of the distinctive features of each Kachina, as Hote, Hototo, Hu', and Soyoko. A fourth group have descriptive names—Angakchina "Long Hair," Wukoqötu "Big Head," Angwusnasomtaqa "One With Crow Tied On," Söhönsomtaqa "One With Grass Tied On." Still others are named after other tribes as Tasap (Navaho) and Yoche (Apache). A sixth group are Kachinas borrowed from other pueblos which bear the names used by the tribe from which they were taken.

The basis for all Kachina impersonation is the mask. The various garments worn as part of the costume and the use of body paint are not limited to Kachina dances, but are used in all Hopi ceremonies. Although certain old masks were made of buckskin or white cotton cloth stretched over a willow frame, most of the masks in use today are of leather. The usual type covers the head completely, fits very snugly, and rests upon the head of the wearer. Tasap Kachina (PLATE XII), Soyal Kachina (PLATE I), and Hote (PLATE XVI) illustrate this type. The other kind only covers the face and is secured by strings tied around the head. Some of these cover the face like Tasap Kachina mana (PLATE XIII) and Poli Kachina (PLATE XXII). Others only extend as far as the mouth, the lower portion of the face being hidden by horsehair, as in Angakchina (PLATE XVI) and Soyoko (PLATE X). There are always two openings about one inch long and a quarter of an inch high through which the wearer looks.

In preparing a mask for use in a dance, it is always scraped clean first. Sometimes the painting and decoration is done by the leader of the kiva, sometimes by the impersonators under his direction. The larger surfaces are covered with paint by squirting it on the mask; the finer lines are applied with a strip of yucca used as a brush. The decoration is very formal and the number of colors, the kind and arrangement of feathers, the elaboration of attachments to the mask give no indication of the relative importance of the Kachina, although the particular combination of them is distinctive for any one. Soyal, Eototo, and Aholi (PLATES I, IV, V) are three of the most important of the Chief Kachinas, yet their masks are least embellished of all. In some the face of the mask is all one color, with just eyes and mouth indicated (PLATES XXII, IV). In others it is divided into two sections by a vertical line with contrasting colors in each section (PLATE XIV). Ahote (PLATE XIX) is divided into two main sections, above and below. The larger surfaces may be decorated with paintings of corn, clouds, falling rain, lightning, circles, stars, or crescents. These are the same symbols used in all Hopi ceremonies, but their position, size, and color all tend to become definitive on the mask of any particular Kachina.

The greatest attention is paid to the painting of the eyes of the mask. The word *posi* in Hopi refers to both eye and seed. In preparing paint for the eyes, watermelon seeds are chewed to generate saliva, which is mixed with the pigment. If the mask has projecting eyes like Hote, Na'tashka, or Ahote (PLATES XVII, XI, XIX) a piece of buckskin is sometimes sewn around a mass of seeds and cotton and then secured to the mask above the eye hole. When the dancers unmask at the Kachina shrine, the paint is always scraped from the eyes first. Eyes are usually represented by rectangular lines around the eye holes, but crescents, circles, and triangles are also used.

Many of the masks have projecting snouts or bills varying in size from that of the Na'tashka (PLATE XI) to a small, tube-shaped bill found in Qa'ö and Navan Kachinas (PLATES XXV, XXIV). These are constructed from a gourd, leather, or wood. Like all parts attached to the mask, they are painted first and secured to the mask afterwards. Teeth are represented by painting and carving the sides and end of the snout, as in Ahote. Soyoko and Hu' Kachina (PLATES X, VII), having no snouts, indicate the teeth by a zigzag line. Ears are sometimes indicated by square disks, as in Navan and Qa'ö Kachinas (PLATES XXIV, XXV). Many Kachinas have horns made of the neck of a gourd cut lengthwise to make them symmetrical. Others have a visor of basketry over the eyes (PLATES XIV XX, XXIV). Horsehair, black or dyed red, is used in Angakchina, Soyoko, Tasap Kachina, and Hahai wuhti (PLATES XVI, X, XII, VIII).

Most Kachina masks are adorned with many feathers, those of the eagle, parrot, owl, spar row hawk, crow, and turkey being most often used. Not only the kind of feather, but whether from the tail, wing, or breast of the bird, whether standing in pairs, arranged fan-wise across the top, or clustered at the side or rear—all of these features are essential for any Kachina.

The collar around the lower edge of the mask is made of evergreen boughs, feathers, an animal skin, dry grass, or buckskin.

Most of the costume worn by the impersonators is of native manufacture. The dancing Kachinas usually wear a kilt woven of white cotton and embroidered with colored woolen yarns along the lower edge and the side border, in symbolic designs of terraced clouds and falling rain. The sash is of the same materials, but it is woven rather than embroidered, and it is worn so that the design on the ends show on the right side of the dancer. Both kilt and sash are tied about the waist at the right side. Some use the white wedding belt with the long knotted fringe instead of the sash, and many have either a belt of silver conches or a Hopi belt of red, green and black wool. Female Kachinas wear belts and sashes tied on the left side. Most wear a fox skin in the rear, inserted in the belt and hanging tail down.

Almost every dancing Kachina has a rattle under the right knee. It is made of a turtle shell and several pieces of sheep's hooves suspended by thongs, and marks the beat with a sharp clicking sound when they dance. Often they have brass bells around the left leg. Moccasins are buckskin, either white, brown or blue. On the left wrist is a silver bow guard, on the right a strand of yarn and a bracelet. Generally, all the silver and turquoise necklaces that are owned or can be borrowed are worn around the neck. Many Kachinas have anklets and armbands.

Practically all dancing Kachinas carry a gourd rattle in the right hand and either a sprig of spruce or a bow and arrows in the left. The other objects carried depend upon the nature of the Kachina. Soyoko has a large knife and a crook, the Na'tashka a saw, Chaveyo a sword, Eototo and Aholi a chief's stick and a netted gourd.

The female figures called Kachinmana (Kachina girls) are always impersonated by men. Their hair is dressed in two large whorls, a style characteristic of unmarried girls before the days of schools and bobbed hair. The rest of the costume is all typical of a Hopi woman's dress—the black dress, white robe with red and black borders, woven belt, and white buckskin moccasins

Exposed portions of the body are covered with paint; the colors used and the manner in which they are applied also serve as distinguishing features of any specific figure.

From an examination of the pictures and this brief analysis of the most prominent features of Kachina impersonation, it is apparent that it is not a realistic art. Although Kachinas are always referred to as human (the Hopi use "he" and "she" when speaking of particular figures), there is no attempt to represent them in human terms. Similarly, those that bear the names of animals are not attempts to represent that particular animal in any specific feature, nor as a whole. What they all possess in common is the basic style of Kachinas as beings of their own genre, differentiated from one another by specific details.

In any particular figure, part of the mask is symbolic and part is ornamental, but it is difficult to draw any line between them. For the most part, the symbols used are common to all Hopi ceremonies, and are found on altars and sand paintings as well as on Kachinas. Feathers are used in making prayer sticks. Prayer feathers hang in the beard of Angakchina (PLATE XVI) and project from the visor of Navan and Hemis Kachinas (PLATES XXIV, XIV). The painted symbols of clouds, rain, lightning, and corn are common to all rites. In short, whatever symbolism is present is of a generalized kind and has no specific connotations.

Although all the figures are illustrated singly, none but the Chief Kachinas appear that way. In the usual dance, a line of from twenty-five to sixty Kachinas, all dressed alike, all masked alike, all singing and dancing in unison, perform for the assembled spectators.

Consequently, it is the effect of the line rather than of the figures composing it that impresses the visitor. Sometimes mixed dances are presented in which the line is made up of many different Kachinas, but even then the synchronization of the line in song and dance creates a unit that the variety of masks and costumes does not destroy.

The usual dance step consists of raising the right foot and stamping the ground with the rhythm of the music. The rattles under the right knee mark the beat. The body is held erect with the arms close to the sides and the hands forward. The major variations on this basic pattern of dancing occur in accordance with changes in the rhythm of the song. Sometimes the entire line will pause, at others two or more steps will be executed in rapid succession. These variations are usually accompanied by gestures with the arms and head—the right arm raised and the head turned in that direction, followed by the same movement of the left arm and the head. Another variation occurs in the turning of the line. At certain points in the song, the entire line changes, but the manner in which the turn is executed tends to be distinctive for each Kachina. Angakchina (PLATE XVI) twists his body half way to the right and then turns completely to the left. Tasap Kachina (PLATE XII) extends the right arm, shakes the rattle, and then turns with the rattle held over the head. Other Kachinas turn one after the other, the movement flowing down the line and back.

These differences in dance steps serve to distinguish one Kachina from another; they become as essential characteristics as the painting and decoration of the mask. But they are just as formal. An Eagle Kachina displays none of the imitative posturing of the actions of the bird that is found in the Eagle Dance. The Hopi do have dances in which the actions of animals and birds are effectively portrayed, but none of the Kachinas bearing animal names ever display this in their dancing.

As in dancing, so in music Kachina songs seem to be differentiated from other kinds of songs. Although there is not enough material dealing with Hopi music by itself, a comparison of western Pueblo music (which includes the Hopi) with that of the eastern Pueblos showed that the former were more specialized and more elaborate, and that the rhythm attained the most complex forms known to date in American Indian music.

Most Kachinas sing their own songs, the only accompaniment being their bells and rattles. However, some have a drummer and some, as Qa'ö Kachina (PLATE XXV), have a chorus to sing for them. This is usually necessary in the lively and more vigorous dances.

When one sees a Kachina dance for the first time, he is not always aware of the variety of songs, for they all seem the same. This is partly due to the muffling effect of the mask, and partly to the fact that each Kachina type has its own style of singing. But as soon as the songs of three different Kachinas are sung without masks it is easy to distinguish them.

Ten to fourteen new songs are composed for each dance, the number of songs determining how many times they will come to dance during the day. Anyone may compose a song. Men who are not taking part often make songs and sing them for the men who are practicing.

In a sense, every song is a prayer, and the words express either the message of the Hopi to the clouds and the Chiefs of the Directions, or the message of the clouds and Kachinas to the Hopi. The same ideas, the same phrases are used over and over in all Kachina songs. In fact, it is really another medium in which the symbols for rain, corn, fertility, and growth are expressed. The sections of the song are broken by the use of vocables.

> Listen, my mothers.
> You have prayed
> That it would rain on your plants.
> Li-i hi-la
> Listen, listen
> Listen, my fathers.
> You have prayed
> That it would rain on your plants.
> Li-i hi-la.
>
> When you look after the rain
> You shall see what you prayed for.
> Li-i hi-la
> When rain falls among your plants
> You shall see pools of water,
> My fathers.
> This is what you prayed for.
> Oho ohowa
> Ihi ihiyi hiho
> Oho hayanani oho hayanani
> Hayanani hayani
> Aha aha ihi ihi
> Ai aihai ihi ihi
> Listen, listen,
> My fathers.
> You prayed for us.
> Yonder, to the west

At the house of Alosaka Chief
We heard.
Happily we prepared.
Many kinds of corn,
Many kinds of clouds
We prepared.
Then we started to come
Along the roads

Made by these old men,
The chiefs.
Aha aha ihi ihi
So, coming from each direction
We shall sprinkle rain.
This is what you prayed for,
My fathers.
Yoho wiya hiya aya

You start smoking your pipe
And hand it to one another.
In the same way [as the clouds of smoke]
The clouds will approach
With rain.
aha ihi aha ihi

The Annual Cycle of Kachinas at Oraibi

THE FIRST OF the masked gods to appear each year is the Soyal Kachina (PLATE I), one of the Chief Kachinas. The day after the Wuwuchim ceremony, at about mid-afternoon, he enters the village from the south side, approaching the kiva in which the Winter Solstice rites are to be held. He totters as he walks, frequently seeming to be on the verge of losing his balance. This peculiarity of his behavior has been interpreted in different ways. Some say that he is very old and feeble; others maintain that the uncertainty of his movement is the result of coming into the bright light of day after having been in the dark so long, for he is the first Kachina to appear since the Home Dance the previous July.

As he approaches the kiva, the people stand around in the plaza and on the house tops, following every move. As he staggers, they involuntarily extend their arms, bend their bodies, and call to him to keep him from falling. Soyal Kachina places the four prayer sticks he has been carrying in his left hand against the edge of the kiva opposite the ladder, takes corn meal from his pouch, and sprinkles it upon them. Then he side-steps around the kiva, throwing meal into the hatchway from each direction. He totters out to the plaza, sprinkles meal upon the shrine, and dances in four places. The song to which he dances cannot be heard, but all the Hopi assert that he "sings in his heart" anyway. He then stumbles out to the western edge of Oraibi, where he is met by a man who gives him a blue prayer stick. After receiving this offering, Soyal Kachina disappears down the side of the mesa. During the entire time, whether dancing or walking, he displays characteristic uncertainty about his balance, causing much amusement and some anxiety lest he fall. His appearance and the placing of the prayer sticks by the kiva serves as an announcement of the approaching Winter Solstice ceremony.

Although this long ceremony is not primarily concerned with the Kachina cult, two other Kachinas appear during the course of its activities. Since this is the time when everything is prepared for the coming year, when they make their road for the future, the big Kachina dances for the spring and early summer are arranged at this time. On the next to the last day, two Mastop Kachinas (PLATE III) prepare in one kiva and emerge during the afternoon. They run around the plaza, give their call, approach some woman and simulate intercourse with her. Then they return to the kiva, carry on a conversation with those inside in a high voice, return and repeat their actions with other women, and go back to the kiva entrance to talk again. They continue to run about until all the women have received their blessing for fertility. When they have finished, they enter the kiva, where they are sprinkled with meal and given prayer sticks. After collecting these offerings from all of the kivas participating in the ceremony, they disappear to deposit them in a shrine.

On the last day, the Kachina season is formally opened by the Qöqölo Kachinas (PLATE III). They are the first to appear as a regular dancing group. There are about twenty as represented in the picture and eight or ten Kachinmanas (female figures), who dance in a line beside them. The manas hold woven plaques containing all kinds of seeds; the others bring presents of all kinds of Hopi foods, which they distribute to the children. They are led about the village and sprinkled with meal by the Powamu Chief. During the course of the afternoon they visit every kiva in the village. At the hatchway they make lines of meal on all four sides. This is called "opening the kivas" and symbolizes the opening of the Kachina season.

The Qöqölo is regarded as something of a clown, and many of the actions on this day are consistent with this characterization. They frequently burlesque the dances of other religious societies, creating a great deal of hilarity. Sometimes, they form two groups and line up and dance as the Snake and Antelope members do in their summer ceremony. Or they may form a circle and do the Basket Dance of the Oaqöl, one of the two women's societies. This is but one of the many occasions in a public dance when the Hopi sense of humor finds expression in burlesque.

From this time on, the Kachinas are thought to be living at their homes nearby, able to visit the people of Oraibi on any occasion. Immediately after the dance of the Qöqölo, each kiva begins to prepare for a series of night dances, most of them coming in January, although they may come after the Powamu rites as well. The preparations for the night dances are not as elaborate as those for the big outdoor dances, for it is only necessary to learn one or two songs for each dance. Since the dances take place in the kivas, it is not practical to have more than twenty-five take part in each dance. The kivas are beehives of activity as the preparations for dances proceed.

In many ways these performances are the most spectacular of all, and it is at this time that the greatest number of masked dances may be seen. In a single night each of the twelve kivas presents a different set of Kachinas, and there are usually three or four nights of dancing. Frequently, these dances are announced by the appearance of a single Koyemsi in the plaza during the day.

About ten o'clock at night, the women, children, and men who are not performing gather in their own kivas. They sit on the raised portion of the floor, leaving the large lower section clear. The only light comes from a small fire on the floor beneath the hatchway which serves as both entrance and smoke vent. It is carefully tended by an old man, the Kiva Chief, who adds just enough fuel to give light and warmth and is generally successful in preventing the smoke from filling the room. The stage is set.

A rattle is heard in the entrance and the stamping of feet upon the roof. The old man calls up, inviting them to come in. A voice answers, usually with some humorous comment, and the dialogue with the unseen visitors continues for some moments. One by one, the Kachinas descend the ladder and take their positions. There may be from sixteen to twenty-five in a group, and the line occupies all the space of the three walls in the lower portion of the kiva. Unless it is a mixed dance, all are masked and costumed alike and arranged according to height, with the tallest figures in the middle and the shortest on the ends. The old man sprinkles the Kachinas with sacred meal, and as he passes the leader in the center of the line, he tells them to begin. The dance is on.

The dance steps, the songs, and the Kachinas are the same that are used in the large dances in the plaza, but the effects are all intensified by the setting. Within that small enclosed space the gods seem to dominate. Nothing else matters. As a Hopi once remarked when we were watching a particularly colorful and vigorous dance, "You don't care about the outside world at all." The pounding of their feet on the floor reverberates, the song fills the kiva with music. The always pronounced rhythm becomes more pronounced. The flickering of the fire creates lighting effects impossible in a modern theatre as it flashes on silver bow guards, on shining black hair, on brightly painted mask, or glistening body paint. Each detail is accentuated for a moment and dropped into shadow again. The Kachinas turn and new colors, new feathers stand out for a moment and then recede to mingle their individual beauty with that of the whole. For it is the whole line performing, the merging of so many details of costume, dance and song, in synchronous movement, that creates such an effective performance. Their numbers seem doubled and trebled by the shadows on walls and ceiling, which assume fantastic forms. Unlike the dances in the plaza that are seen from above, here the gods must be looked up at—perhaps a more fitting point of view. All too soon the leader's rattle is extended and they stop. Slowly they ascend the ladder while the old man sprinkles each with meal and throws a little up the hatchway after them.

But this is only the first act. Again feet are heard on the roof and rattle sounds in the opening. A new group enters and dances. They may have a Koyemsi with them to beat a drum and to make amusing comments. Once I saw a set of Chakwaina Kachinas dance in the kiva. Unlike most Kachinas, they dance with both feet, very rapidly, and turn by jumping around and bending down until both hands almost touch the floor. It was a lively and vigorous dance. The spectators' attention was captured by the leading figure of the line. He was so small that his feet barely reached from one rung of the ladder to the next when he entered, but he compensated for his lack of size by the zest with which he danced. Everyone was delighted with his performance. The Koyemsi became jealous and shouted, "I am the one you are supposed to laugh at," provoking even more mirth.

A second groups leaves and is succeeded by a third. In all, twelve different dance groups perform in the kiva, and each group dances once in each kiva. Often it is dawn before they finish their rounds. In later years, when less than half the number of kivas participated, each group made the circuit twice.

There are usually three or four night dances during the winter months, so that from thirty to fifty dancing Kachinas are seen at this time. About the beginning of February— actually, at the appearance of the new moon called Powamuyao—night dances are suspended for the duration of the long Powamu ceremony. This is the first of the major rites connected with the Kachina cult.

During this ceremony, when initiations take place, children learn the secrets of the Kachina cult. It is also the occasion for the appearance of certain Chief Kachinas, whose acts will be described. The general purpose of the whole ceremony is purification, and like all of the long rites, it involves many magical acts designed to produce rain and abundant crops in the season to come. One of the special features is the growth of bean and corn plants in the kivas for sixteen days. They are planted in boxes and trays, watered regularly, and forced by maintaining a constant high temperature. On the last day the fresh young plants are brought into the plaza by the Kachinas and the wonderful effect created upon the uninitiated can be imagined. If the plants grow well, it is a sign of a successful crop during the coming summer. Each of the last four mornings, four Pachavuhu Kachinas visit all of the kivas and examine the plants to see that none of the stems are broken.

The leading officers are the Powamu Chief and the Kachina Chief. At the proper time they take prayer sticks to all of the kivas, which is an announcement that it is time to plant the beans. That night the Powamu Chief again visits each kiva and blesses the planting by smoking over it and sprinkling it with meal.

On the morning of the fifth day, only in the years when the children's initiation is held, the following rites take place. A special altar is set up for the initiation. Many sacred objects are arranged on a ridge of damp sand, and at both sides are slabs with paintings of the Hu' Kachinas, the whippers (PLATE VII). At one side is a symbolic sand painting made of different colored sands. When all is ready, children between the ages of six and ten are brought into the kiva by their sponsors. Each throws a little corn meal toward the altar and is seated at one end of the kiva. Each novice is given a perfect ear of white corn, referred to as his "Corn Mother."

They sit around the altar, smoke over it, and sing a series of sacred songs during which an eagle feather is tied to the top of everybody's head. After the ancients have been summoned from the six directions by the Kachina Chief, they all rush up the ladder. The children inside hear shouts and a great deal of running around up above. All return, followed by the Chowilawu Kachina (not represented). His body is covered with white kaolin, daubed with black on the forearms, lower legs, the back, and the breast. His kilt is made of horsehair dyed red and suspended from a green leather belt. His mask has a cloud and rain design on the forehead, terraced cloud design for ears, and a bunch of eagle feathers on top. In his hands he carries a plaque made of many semi-circular leaves hinged in the center. As he dances, he opens and closes the various leaves, revealing painted symbols of rain, clouds, corn, and lightning. He goes at once to the sand painting and executes a jumping dance around its border, opening and closing the leaves of the plaque as he dances. All during this time the leaders sprinkle him with corn meal and water and wave sacred objects from the altar in his direction. When he stops dancing, both chiefs give him prayer sticks and meal and he disappears up the ladder accompanied by the others. There is the same shouting and commotion that preceded his appearance.

When the men return, the Powamu Chief addresses the children, telling them under no circumstances to tell anyone what the have seen, not even their fathers and mothers. If asked about Chowilawu, they are to say the light was bad and they could not see. Finally, they are warned that the Kachinas will punish them should they fail to keep the secret. These boys are now members of the Powamu society, and they will lead the Kachinas about the plaza, sprinkle them with meal, and answer the words of their songs. The girls are also initiated so that they know the secret of the cult, but with few exceptions they play only a minor role in the Kachina performances.

The following day the initiation into the Kachina society takes place in a different kiva. Two sand paintings are made. One is a representation of Angwusnasomtaqa (PLATE VI) with two Hu' Kachinas (PLATE VII) beside her. All are shown holding yucca whips. At one corner of this large painting is a smaller one representing the colors of the six directions with the Hopi path extending to the east. In one corner, an enclosure is made with blankets behind which four Koyemsi Kachinas are concealed.

All the children who were initiated into Powamu the previous day are now present, but only as spectators. The children who are to be inducted into the Kachina division are brought in by their sponsors and a rite to promote their growth is conducted. The Kachina Chief and his assistant stand by the ladder holding trays containing prayer sticks and sacred meal. Then the Powamu Chief enters, wearing a white wedding robe, carrying a gourd filled with water in his left hand. He also has a crook with ears of corn and packets of corn meal tied to it. According to Voth, he represents the god of germination, and when asked where he comes from and for what purpose, he makes the following speech

"Those there at Towanashape were all assembled making a ladder. They put up the ladder; with turquoise strands was it tied together. That way we came up and out. Eastward we came, traveling on a road marked with yellow corn seed. We beheld the house of the Akush Kachina Chief. In a beautiful yellow mist was the house enveloped So we went in. The Akush Kachina Chief was there. He has beautiful yellow corn seed, beans, watermelons, muskmelons, and that way he lives Here these Oraibi children, little girls, little boys, of different size here at the sipapu shall they know our ceremonies; yes, they shall know them. Beautiful ladder beam, beautifuL ladder rungs, tied the beam with turquoise strands. Thus, we came out.

"Westward we came. On a road marked with beautiful blue corn seed we traveled. We beheld the house of the Nakyachok Kachina Chief. Beautiful blue mist enveloped the house. Thus, we went in. The Nakyachok Kachina Chief was there. He has beautiful blue corn seeds. . ."

This paragraph is a repetition of the one preceding except that blue is the color used throughout. Then, for each of the following Kachina Chiefs, the whole speech is repeated except for the direction in which they travel and the color. Westward to Hototo—red; southward to Mastop—white; northward to Söhönsomtaqa—black; westward to Hu'— variegated colors; eastward to Achamali (a shrine near Oraibi) the home of Hahai wuhti—many colors; southward to Palakwai—many colors; south to Eototo and Aholi— many colors. It concludes as follows with the arrival of the Kachinas at Oraibi after their long journey.

"Northward we came. On a road marked with beautiful corn seed of different colors did we travel. We beheld the houses of Shokhungyoma, Koyongainiwa, Lomankwaima. A beautiful mist enveloped the houses. Thus, we entered. Shokbungyoma was there,

Koyongainiwa was there, Lomankwaima was there. They had beautiful corn seed of different colors, beans, watermelons, muskmelons, and thus they lived. Here these Oraibi children, little girls, little boys, of different sizes, here at the sipapu shall they know our ceremonies. Yes, they shall know them. Beautiful ladder beam, beautiful ladder rungs, fastened to the ladder with turquoise. Thus, we came out.

"And now you gather your people, your children, all of them into your lap and hold them all very fast. But now this time open your hand to these people that this yucca may enlighten their hearts, and when their hearts have been enlightened here their heads will be bathed with the roots of this yucca and then they will be done.

"And thus, then follow to the white rising and to the yellow rising this road marked with nice corn pollen and on which these four old age marks are standing. On them you will support yourselves, and over yonder, where the shortest one stands, may you fall asleep as old men and old women. But I am not wandering alone. Here at the comer they already have arrived (the four Koyemsi behind the blanket in the comer). Come in, be welcome."

Finishing his long speech, the Powamu Chief goes to the children and sprinkles them with water from his gourd. Meanwhile the Koyemsis have come out from behind the blanket. When the Powamu Chief leaves the kiva, the Koyemsis walk around the smaller sand painting four times and finally stop, one on each side of it. The one on the north side picks up the corn ear and stone celt and touches each candidate with them and then returns them to their position on the sand painting. Those on the east, south, and west sides do the same in turn, and then disappear behind the blanket.

The long speech, the sprinkling, and the acts of ritual described all build up to a tremendous climax. A feeling of tension pervades the kiva. The children have been looking at the large sand painting of the whipping Kachinas on the floor and know what is in store for them. Suddenly, a great commotion is heard above—rattles and hells sound, the call of the dreaded Hu' Kachina comes down through the opening. There is tramping and beating on the roof of the kiva. Finally, they enter, two Hu' Kachinas (PLATE VII) and Angwusnasomtaqa (PLATE VI). The latter is a figure of great dignity. In her hands she holds a number of whips of yucca blades tied together at the base. She takes a position at one corner of the large sand painting and the whippers stand at its edge on both sides of her.

While they are taking up their positions, they wave their whips so that they swish through the air, grunt, give their call, and jump around so that the bells and rattles add their noise to the general hubbub. The boys who are to be whipped and their sponsors wear no clothing. The girls are whipped fully dressed. One sponsor leads a boy out so that they are both standing upon the sand painting and holds up his hands while the Hu' Kachina whips him with the yucca lashes. There is no feeling that this ordeal must be born

meal. Then, he goes to deposit the offerings in the shrine. All of these Kachinas wear sprigs of spruce on their armbands and under their belts. Pieces of spruce are broken off by the members of the Powamu society, are smoked over in the kiva, and later distributed to the houses, where they are placed upon the seed corn for the spring planting.

During the afternoon a procession of Kachinas is led into the plaza by He'e'e (PLATE IX), the warrior maid Kachina. She visits the shrines around Oraibi that are regarded as the homes of certain Chief Kachinas, and each of them joins her as she moves toward the village. There are nine of these Kachinas in the line, but none of these are represented in the plates. As they pass each kiva, more Kachinas come out and join them, running around the plaza until the village is full of them. I once saw more than one hundred Kachinas appear at this celebration. After the Kachinas have been in the plaza for some time, He'e'e leads the procession back along the same route. As the Kachinas come to their kivas they go in, so that by the time the edge of the village is reached only the Chief Kachinas remain. These go to their own shrines.

Most years this procession ends the public appearance of the masked gods during the Powamu ceremony. However, every four or five years this procession is more elaborate and is called the Pachavu ceremony. This occurs whenever men have been initiated into the four Wuwuchim societies the previous November. Then the line is made up of the follow- ing figures: the Powamu Chief leads, carrying a basket tray containing prayer sticks, fol- lowed by four Chief Kachinas walking abreast and singing throughout their march; behind them came a dozen Bean Maidens, one from each kiva, bearing empty trays. Beside the line walks Hahai wuhti (PLATE VIII), sprinkling water from her gourd on the children, acting silly, distributing gifts of food, and speaking in a high falsetto voice. They line up by the Powamu kiva and are blessed with smoke, meal, and medicine in the same way Eototo and Aholi were in the morning. Then they march out of the village.

That night, every year, the unmasked bean dance occurs in all the kivas. Everyone who has been initiated goes to his own kiva just as he does for the night dances. It is at this time that the recently initiated see unmasked dancing, for the men who dance are called Powamu Kachinas, even though they wear no masks. The male figures wear all the usual paraphernalia of dancing Kachinas—kilts, sashes, belts, turtle shell rattles, moccasins and anklets. Quantities of turquoise beads are around their necks. In the right hand is a gourd rattle and in the left a sprig of spruce. The bodies are painted red, yellow, and blue in a pre- scribed manner. On their heads are imitation squash blossoms fashioned from corn husks.

The female figures are impersonated by men, wearing women s clothing—black dress, white buckskin moccasins, belt, and the maiden's blanket. Their hair is done up at the sides in whorls like those on the Hemis Kachinmana (PLATE XV). The last of the female figures is dressed in old clothes and wears a comical false face mask. She carries on a protracted and humorous conversation with the leader inside from the kiva opening before entering.

There is one group like this from every kiva, and each group dances once in all kivas. This arrangement is like the night dances, but the form of the dance is different. The male figures line up at one side, the female at the other, the ends of both lines meeting at the far end of the kiva. It is essentially a square dance set. The male and female at the far end take hands, dance forward and back, forward and separate to take places at the near ends of their respective lines. The next couple follows them, and each line progresses circularly. The dance lasts about twenty minutes, and the dancers leave to be succeeded by another group and the whole performance is repeated until the circuit has been completed.

Ordinarily the bean dance concludes the Powamu rites, but when the Pachavu is held there is one more day of Kachina processions. In the morning, He'e'e leads in the line of Chief Kachinas as on the previous day. However, one of them carries a number of long willow sticks upon his back. Again as they pass each kiva, many Kachinas emerge until the plaza is full of them. All of the Kachinas known as scare Kachinas—generally they have protruding eyes and big teeth—are furnished with willow whips as they run around the plaza. Periodically during the day, He'e'e rushes to the housetop and waves her arm in a wide arc. This is a signal to the Kachinas, who chase everyone into the houses with their whips, beating anyone who fails to seek refuge inside. All doors are closed and all windows are covered with blankets. While the people are held, the bean plants are cut in the kivas and taken to a shrine south of Oraibi. After the bearers of the plants have disappeared, the people gradually come back to the plaza to watch the antics of the Kachinas, only to be driven back to the houses again when He'e'e runs to the roof and waves her arm. This is repeated until all of the beans have been cut and taken south of Oraibi.

At the shrine the bean plants are arranged on a frame and placed on trays to be carried by the Bean Maidens. There is one Bean Maiden from each kiva and usually one Kachina to help her carry the tray. These Kachinas are of many different kinds, but never scare Kachinas. The procession lines up in the following order: Village Chief, Crier, Powamu Chief, Eototo, Aholi, He'e'e and the twelve Bean Maidens and their assisting Kachinas. The other Kachinas are grouped roughly around the Bean Maiden from their own kiva.

This long line slowly comes into sight from the south side of the village and makes its way to the place where the prayer stick is set in a hole in the plaza. Here each tray of beans is set down on each side of the hole for a moment. The procession then goes to the Powamu kiva, goes around it four times, and waits until the members come Out to bless them in the usual way with smoke, prayer sticks, and medicine. Then the Kachinas all return to their own kivas, and the maidens take the beans home to be distributed among their friends for use in the evening feast.

Frequently, many of the Kachinas accompanying the procession have carrying baskets on their backs full of young bean plants. As they move through the plaza, they stagger under their loads and sometimes topple over backwards from the weight of their burdens. All of this foreshadows the time of the next harvest when the Hopi will likewise stagger under the load of their abundant crops. It also adds a bit of amusement to the otherwise dignified procession, for each Kachina stays in character throughout the afternoon. Kwikwilyaqa (PLATE XXVII) follows the others around, trying to mimic all their actions, Hubuwa (PLATE XXVI) runs around cross-legged, and each accentuates his own idiosyncrasies.

The last two days' activities are something of a miracle for the uninitiated. At this time of year it is still cold, snow is often on the ground, and yet the masked gods bring trays and baskets of freshly grown young bean plants.

Every year, usually in January, the Soyoko group of Kachinas appears and makes the round of all the houses, disciplining the children. They are feared by the children, who are all familiar with the stories of Soyoko, who catches Hopi boys and girls to cook and eat or feed to her own children. Parents often threaten their disobedient children by telling them of Soyoko, and this annual appearance of the whole group reinforces the threats.

The Soyoko (PLATE X) is the leader of the group. She is accompanied by two Na'tashka (PLATE XI), one as represented, the other having a black mask and an equally large bill. Another terrifying figure with a black mask, big mouth, and feathers running from front to back, referred to as their uncle, makes the rounds with them. The group is completed by two Heheya Kachinas who carry lariats, and rope anyone who ventures too close to them.

The children are warned in advance by their parents that these monsters are coming to take away all who are disobedient. When they appear in the village, they give the low rumbling call and approach the nearest house. The Na'tashka go up to the walls and scrape the ends of their saws against them. The uncle calls for the child and accuses him of all his misdeeds. Sometimes he threatens to take the child away with him. The Soyoko repeats the threats, often reaching out toward him with her crook. By this time the child is usually terrified, clings to his mother's skirts, and attempts to hide behind her. At this point, presents of corn meal are offered to the monsters. The uncle reaches for them and takes the child's arm instead. Despite promises of good behavior, the Kachinas are adamant. The exchange of pleas and threats is quite protracted, and throughout, the others are giving their low rumbling call, banging their saws against the house, and jumping around to the accompaniment of their bells and rattles. Finally, the uncle agrees to relent provided the present offered is satisfactory to the long-billed Na'tashkas. They always refuse three times, greater quantities of food being offered after each refusal. Finally, they accept it. Then it is offered to the two Heheya Kachinas to taste. If it meets with their approval, it is loaded into a carrying basket, and they move on to the next house. Here the whole scene is reenacted. In this way, they visit every house in the village, and finally go away with their baskets filled with meat and corn meal.

The Dance

Iɴ ᴛʜᴇ sᴘʀɪɴɢ and early summer, great day-long dances occur. Although Oraibi probably does not have more than three such dances each year, every village presents two or three, so that there are about twenty Kachina dances on the reservation from May to July. Primarily, like all ceremonies, the dance is religious. It is for rain. But it is much more. It combines music, dance, and ornamentation in one art form, providing the Hopi with their greatest esthetic satisfaction. It is the occasion for the display of their hospitality to visitors. It is the end point of days of economic activity. It offers an opportunity to show their affection for their children by the gifts anonymously given by the Kachinas. It is the time when the clowns present their burlesques for the amusement of the assembled spectators. It is a holiday. But it is all one experience to the Hopi, and he succinctly includes all these activities in the single word, *tikive*—"the dance day."

For sixteen nights before the dance, the men who take part go to the kiva every night to practice, learn their songs, and prepare their masks. Anyone who has been initiated may take part, so there are usually from forty to sixty men involved. For days the women of the family asking for the dance are busy grinding corn meal, making piki, and preparing other kinds of food for those who take part in the dance. And the last two days everyone is busy preparing feast dishes, butchering sheep, or making dolls for the children in some place hidden from their view. The last night the dancers stay up all night in the kiva. Those who asked for the dance must also stay up all night grinding corn meal. The members of the Powamu fraternity, who will conduct the Kachinas around the plaza the next day, are busy making prayer sticks for them. Shortly before dawn, the dancers come into the plaza and dance once, unmasked.

Everyone is up at sunrise, washing hair, dressing in the best clothes, donning the brightest shawls. In every house in Oraibi the cloth is spread upon the floor and quantities of the specially prepared feast dishes are set out, for on dance day the home village is host to visitors from all the other Hopi towns. From early morning until noon the roads leading to the village carry a steady stream of visitors in trucks, on horseback, in wagons, and on foot. No Hopi who can possibly attend misses a Kachina dance.

The Kachinas dance the first time shortly after sun up. The long line is led into the plaza by their "father," who makes a road of corn meal for them to follow. He lines them up on one side of the plaza, sprinkles the leader with meal, and gives the signal for them to begin. When they have finished, he leads them to the end of the plaza, where they dance again. The third position is along the side of the plaza opposite the first. In each position they dance to the same song, which is sung twice. Finally, they are led out of the plaza to their resting place, where they stay for half an hour or so. When they return to dance again, they sing a new song, and during the course of the day usually dance twelve or fourteen times.

Each time they leave the plaza, the men in the home village circulate among the visitors and invite their friends and relatives to their homes, where they are fed. There they stay eating and exchanging pleasant small talk until there is a cry, "They're coming." Immediately everyone leaves and seeks a vantage point on the roof or in front of the houses from which to watch the dance.

One of the most popular Kachinas for these dances is the Tasap Kachina (PLATE XII). There are about forty figures masked and costumed as shown, and perhaps fifteen Tasap Kachina manas (PLATE XIII). The latter dance in a line parallel to the others and close to them. Besides these Kachinas, there is a single side dancer, referred to as the Yeibichai, or the Kachinas' grandfather. His mask is white with eyes and mouth indicated by a few black lines forming a rectangle. A corn stalk is painted in the center of the face of the mask and there is a fringe of red horse hair on the forehead. A few eagle tail feathers stand up at the back of the mask. He wears a velvet shirt, almost any kind of trousers, moccasins and buckskin leggings with silver buttons on the side. Around the waist is a belt of large silver conches. Over his right shoulder and under his left arm is tied a large white buckskin that hangs down behind him. In his left hand he carries a very small bow and arrows, and a skin pouch full of corn meal.

The presence of the Yeibichai is in large measure responsible for the popularity of this dance. He dances back and forth outside the line of Kachinas, using a very complicated series of steps. When he is not dancing, he pantomimes the words of the song. He walks with a great swagger. When the Kachinas are lined up ready to dance, he gives the signal by running from one end of the line to the other, giving his hooting call, running down the line to the central figure and dropping some corn meal beside it. Like the "father," he constantly walks along the line, sprinkling the Kachinas with meal.

About noon, the clowns usually come out, five of them appearing on the housetops, and falling all over themselves as they clamber down the ladders and make their way into the plaza. They are naked except for a breech cloth and often wear fur caps. Their bodies are covered with paint. As soon as they appear, women come out of the houses bearing enormous quantities of food of all kinds, which the clowns pile up in the center of the plaza. All day they stuff themselves with food and squabble with one another over small bits. The exhibition of gluttony is a constant feature of the clowns' behavior and always provokes laughter. They talk constantly, the more ridiculous the content of their conversation the better. All of the rules of etiquette, the proprieties of social intercourse, the moderation of daily life in speech and behavior are flouted by the clowns. The reversal of all the normalities of Hopi life in a series of excesses seems to be the essence of their humor.

When the Kachinas are dancing, the clowns, too, sprinkle them with meal. They address the Kachinas with foolish questions, only to receive the Kachinas' hoot or call in reply. They carry on long conversations with the Yeibichai, who always answers in pantomime. When the Kachinas leave the plaza, the clowns indulge in mock dramatizations of myths, crawling through hoops and then acting as if they had been transformed into some animal.

But probably the most effective of all their antics are the burlesques. During the absence of the dancers from the plaza, special groups of clowns, wearing grotesque masks and clothing in keeping with the character impersonated, enter the plaza. Sometimes they are Navajos, sometimes they stage a mock Hopi wedding, sometimes they ridicule government officials and school teachers. One of the most humorous that I have seen was a take-off of the behavior of the swarms of tourists who invade the villages for the Snake Dance each year. First several clowns ran into the plaza carrying small black boxes, and then proceeded to "take pictures" of everything in sight and from every imaginable angle. They even dragged people out of the houses and made them assume ridiculous poses. Then they settled themselves on the housetops, removed their shirts, and exhibited all the manifestations of restlessness seen on such occasions. Finally, a clown entered at the far end of the plaza and immediately called in a loud voice to another sitting at the opposite end. They carried on a conversation in English and at the top of their lungs. The new arrival strode across the plaza, made a great fuss as he clambered up the ladder, and then they indulged in a great deal of hand shaking and back slapping.

By afternoon the plaza is crowded. Now, as the Kachinas come in each time, they are laden with presents—dolls in their own image, bows and arrows painted and decorated with feathers, rolls of different colored piki, melons, baked corn, and baskets of peaches. They set their presents down in the center of the plaza and line up to dance. This offers the Yeibichai an opportunity to display his virtuosity, as he dances among the presents and hops over them on one foot. Sometimes the clowns try to imitate him. When the Kachinas have moved to the second position, they step out of line, pick up their presents, and look for the child for whom it is intended. After giving the present, each Kachina returns to the line. They dance in the other two positions and retire to rest.

Each time they come back,they sing a new song, reiterating their prayer for rain. During the dance their "father" answers the words of their song, and shouts to encourage them.

> Aba ihi aha ihi
> At last we came there,
> To our houses.
> Blue prayer sticks
> You offered us.
> The chiefs of all directions
> Prepared the good life.

> Those living in each direction
> Have asked us,
> "Our fathers what do they say?
> How shall our fathers send them there?"
> Yes, yes
> We shall soon visit them with rain.
> Yes, yes
> We shall soon come to them with rain.
> Awiya hiyana awiya hiyana
> Aba ihi ihi aha
> Aha ihi ihi aha

Indeed, they said
You should go yonder.
With that shall we start
With rain from all directions
Falling upon their plants.
Aha ihi aha ihi

Listen, my fathers.
Listen, listen, my friends.
Don't lose faith in me.
Pray to me.
I, in reply, With water downpouring
Will keep you alive.
So, go yonder to the west.
On the wings of male turkeys [prayer sticks]
The clouds will appear.
This way, my animals [eagles]
Will bring rain
On their flapping wings.
Owa iloi
Aha aha iloi aha
Aba ihi ihi.

After the Kachinas have danced for the last time, their "father" addresses them with a speech embodying the prayers of the Hopi, gives them all prayer sticks, and leads them out of the village to the Kachina shrine. There each man unmasks, plants the prayer stick, and makes a road of meal toward the San Francisco Peaks for the Kachinas to travel home.

The Niman Kachina Ceremony

THIS IS THE second major rite of the Kachina cult, and like the first, consists of eight days of secret activity in the kiva followed by a public dance on the ninth day. The Kachina Chief and the Powamu Chief are the leaders, assisted by members of the Powamu society. This group conducts all the secret rites— the making and planting of prayer sticks, setting up the altar, singing the songs of sequence, and using all the usual procedures of Hopi ceremonial.

This secret part is arranged so that the final dance occurs about the middle of July. The dancers are a second group, practicing during the time that the others are conducting their rites before the altar. The privilege of dancing in the Home Dance rotates annually among all the kivas. Their preparation is similar to that for any outdoor dance, but it is customary to present the Hemis Kachina (PLATES XIV and XV) on this occasion, although some other Kachina may be substituted.

The purpose of the ceremony is to celebrate the departure of the Kachinas from the village to their home in the San Francisco Mountains. After this dance, the masked gods appear no more until a new annual cycle starts with a new year.

In addition to the usual preparations for a Kachina dance, messengers are sent to Kisiwu, fifty miles north of Oraibi, and there they plant prayer sticks. When they return, they bring many spruce boughs, which are worn in the armbands and under the belts of the Hemis Kachina. The first corn is generally harvested for Home Dance.

When the Kachinas come to the plaza to dance for the first time, just after sunrise, they bring armsful of corn. On this occasion the whole plant is uprooted and bundles of them—ears, leaves, stalks—are distributed to the people of the village. In addition to one or two "fathers" to make their road and conduct them around the plaza, the Kachina Chief is present. He is barefooted, dressed in just kilt and sash, his hair down his back, and carrying a sack of meal and a prayer stick. All day long he fasts.

In the Home Dance there are no clowns, no side dancers, just the two lines of Kachinas. The longer line of Hemis Kachinas always dances toward the houses, the Kachina manas next to them, but on the side nearest the center of the plaza. As they dance, the end figure starts to turn, and as he completes his turn the next one starts. Gradually, one by one, the Kachinas dance about until they face in the opposite direction. In the execution of this turn the Kachina manas go in the opposite direction, so that it gives the impression of their being turned by a series of meshed gears. After the entire line has turned, they start reversing the process down the line until they are back in their original position. As they turn, the different symbols painted on the back of the flat superstructure surmounting the mask are revealed; the familiar symbols of corn, clouds, rain, lightning appear once more.

When the first song has been sung, the Kachinas take a different position. The Hemis Kachinas face toward the center of the plaza, side by side, with the last few figures at each end moving forward a little so that the line is curved in at the ends. Sheepskins and blankets are spread before the central figures, and the Kachina manas kneel upon them with their backs to the plaza. They place their gourds upon the ground, rest a notched stick upon the gourd, and scrape it with a scapula. This provides the basic accompaniment to the song. They start rubbing the stick slowly and gradually increase the tempo. After sixteen strokes, the Kachinas start their song. There is no change of position while they are in this formation, but the use of the rattles is quite complicated. The turtle shell rattles under the right knee and the gourd rattles held in the right hand do not sound simultaneously. Instead, the former are used in the usual way, but the latter are shaken in double time. Toward the end of the song, the Kachina manas rise, the fathers of the Kachinas take the blankets and robes, and they finish the dance in the same formation as in the beginning.

These two distinct parts of the dance are used on each of the plaza, and then the Kachinas are led out. Because of the length of the dance, the Hemis Kachinas only dance eight times during the day. Like other Kachinas, they bring presents to the children and distribute them, but all of the comic by-play is absent.

Toward evening, they are led to the kiva in which the altar has been set up. Here they dance for the last time. When they have finished, members of the Powamu society, both men and women, dressed in kilts and sashes or ceremonial robes, emerge from the kiva.

One smokes upon each Kachina, another sprinkles each with medicine, and the others place prayer sticks and sacred meal in their left hands. When all have received their offerings, the father of the Kachinas addresses them with a speech, as follows:

"Indeed, it is like this.
After all, I set the date
For you at this time.
The sun has come
To the appointed place.
Therefore, you will return.

At your homes
Your fathers,
Your mothers,
Your people,
Are awaiting you.
So, you will start
To carry our words to them.

Listen.
We, here,
Have worked all day for you.
You have voiced our prayers.
We are tired.
You, too, are tired.
When you arrive at your homes,
These words of ours
You will give to them.

Soon, you will come from there
To bring us drink.
Around here
Our crops, our plants
Are growing poorly.
You will come soon

To bring them drink,
When you have brought them drink,
When they have drunk,
When their children have grown,
When they have eyes,
When our children, the little ones, taste them
They will surely be happy.
Therefore, you will come soon
To bring us drink.

If we drink
All the people
Will live happily.
Then, our lives
Will reach old age.
With our children
Our lives will be enjoyed
To old age.
This is why
You will take our words to them.

As soon as it rains
Green things will grow.
Game animals,
Jack rabbits,
Cottontails,
Will feed on these greens
And will increase.
Then, these eagles,
Our animals,
Will grow here with their children.
When the children of these eagles have grown

We shall gather them on our houses,
Raising them here.
With their downy feathers
We shall beautify ourselves
For our fathers in each direction.

Like this it will be.
So, you, with strength,
Happily will go home."

As the father finishes his speech, he sprinkles them all with meal and then makes a road for them toward the west. Slowly, they follow after him. Everyone stands looking after the last of the Kachinas, their feathers ruffled by an occasional wind, as they file out of the village. No one moves to go home until the last Kachina is out of sight. for they all know the masked gods won't come again for half a year.

Notes

All Hopi names have been written as far as possible with English letters. The one exception is ö, pronounced as in German, schön. The other vowels approximate the quality of the following English words:

a as in father   *o* as in note

e as in met   *u* as in put

i as in pique

The consonants p, t, k are not aspirated as in English. The digraph *ch* is pronounced as in English church. The digraph *ng* is pronounced as in English sing.

All references to other publications listed in the bibliography are by number.

The most detailed study is Fewkes' (5), illustrated by 190 drawings by Hopi artists. This was preceded by an earlier and briefer study (4). An excellent study of the Kachina cult at Zuni, the nearest Pueblo neighbors of the Hopi, is Bunzel's (i). Although Kachina dancing has been reported from all of the southwestern pueblos except Taos, it is only at the Hopi villages and Zuni that it occupies such a prominent place in the life of the people. It is only at these places that visitors are permitted to witness these dances.

Both of Fewkes' studies are based on information obtained at Walpi, on the eastern mesa. Stephen (8) contains a great deal of detailed information on all Hopi ceremonies, but it too, is based largely on Walpi practices; pp. 155-576 deal with Kachinas.

p. 8 The construction, painting, and decoration of masks is described in (8) pp. 167, 169 to 170, 171, 212, 215-216, 312,381,382, 395-396, 519.

p. 11 Discussion on music is based on (6).

p. 12 The song was recorded in Hopi and translated.

p. 15 Soyal Kachina's appearance is mentioned in (2) p. 14, and described in (8), p 3, note 5. Plate V and VI in (2) show the Kachina and his prayer sticks.

p. 16 Mastop Kachina's actions are described in (2) p. 45, and the mask is illustrated in plates XXIII, XXIV, XXV of the same publication.

p. 16 Qöqölo Kachinas ate described in (2) p. 58, and illustrated in plates XXVI, XXVII, XXXI, XXXII, XXXIII, XXXIV.

p. 18 The description of the Powamu Ceremony is based on Voth's account (9), supplemented by my own information. (9) describes the entire ceremony in detail.

p. 19 The Powamu initiation is described in (9) pp. 91, 92. Chowilawu is illustrated in plate Ll.

p. 20 The long speech is quoted from (g) pp. 99-101. Voth gives the Hopi from which he translated this in an appendix. The speech names the places with which various Chief Kachinas are associated, and also indicates the Hopi association of specific colors with each of the six directions. The names Sholthungyoma, Koyongainiwa, and Lomankwaima refer to the men who held office in this ceremony at the time Voth saw it. The Koyemsi are illustrated in (5) plate XLV.

p. 20 The sand paintings for the Kachina initiation are shown in (9) plates LII, LIII, LIV.

p. 21 The whipping is described (9) pp. 103-104 and illustrated in plate LXIII.

p. 24 Voth did not see the Pachavu ceremony. This account is based on my own observations at Shungopavi in 1935 and information obtained at Oraibi.

p. 26 The Soyoko group is described in (5) pp. 70-75, and illustrated in plates IX, X, Xll. At Oraibi they are described in (9) p. 118.

p. 29 Many of the outdoor Kachina dances are described in (7) and (8) pp. 353-492. This section also contains several descriptions of the antics of Hopi clowns.

p. 30 The Yeibichai is described in (5) p. 98, plate XXXVI.

p. 32 The song was recorded in Hopi and translated.

p. 35 The Niman Kachina Ceremony is described in (8), pp. 493-575. It is also discussed by Fewkes in (3) which deals with the Second Mesa villages as well as Walpi.

p. 37 The speech is one of several recorded in Hopi and translated.

Selected Bibliography

BUNZEL, RUTH L.

1932   *Zuni Katcinas.* Bureau of American Ethnology, 47th Annual Report,
         pp. 837-1086.
         The most complete account of the Kachina cult at Zuni, the pueblo located most
         closely to the Hopi villages. Contains 60 plates in black and white, illustrating
         most of the known Kachinas.

COLTON, HAROLD S.

1949   *Hopi Kachina Dolls.* Albuquerque: University of New Mexico Press. 15) pp.
         A detailed study of the small carved and painted wooden figurines made in
         likeness of the Kachinas. Identifies and classifies 250 beings with drawings and
         color plates.

DOCKSTADER, FREDERICK J.

1954   *The Kachina and the White Man.* Bloomfield Hills, Michigan: Cranbrook Institute
         of Science. 185 pp.
         A study of the impact of white contact upon the Hopi Kachina cult. Illustrated
         with 16 color plates and 23 line drawings.

FEWKES, JESSE W.

1894   *Dolls of the Tusayan Indians.* Leiden: Internati. Archiv für Ethnologie, vol II,
         pp. 45-73.
         One of the first studies of Hopi Kachina dolls, illustrated with color plates.

1897   *Tusayan Katcinas.* Bureau of American Ethnology, 15th Annual Report,
         pp. 245-313.
         A brief account of the Kachinas at First Mesa, illustrated with color plates and
         half-tone photographs.

1898   *The Growth of Hopi Ritual.* Journal of American Folklore, Vol. XI, pp. 173-194.
        A study of the development of Hopi ceremonial customs and the origin of
        the Kachinas.

1901   *An Interpretation of Katcina Worship.* Journal of American Folklore, vol. XIV,
        pp. 81-94.
        An early interpretation of the rationale affecting the growth of the Kachina cult.

1903   *Hopi Katcinas, Drawn by Native Artists.* Bureau of American Ethnology, 21st
        Annual Report, pp. 3-126.
        The most detailed study to date of Kachinas at First Mesa, illustrated with more
        than 200 color drawings. A few deal with ceremonial figures other than Kachinas.

PARSONS, ELSIE CLEWS (editor)
1925   *A Pueblo Indian Journal, 1920-1921.* American Anthropological Association,
        Memoir #32, 123 pp.
        A diary kept by a First Mesa man focused on the round of annual events in the
        village. Contains black and white drawings of Kachinas, and some photographs
        of dances.

1936   *Hopi Journal of Alexander M. Stephen.* New York: Columbia University Press,2 vols.
        Pages 155-570 describes Kachina dances and ceremonies at Walpi during the
        years 1888-1894. Contains many line drawings of masks, and some illustrations
        in color.

1939   *Pueblo Indian Religion.* Chicago: University of Chicago Press, 2 vols. Pp. 501-510
        and 766-778 concerns Hopi Kachina dances and ceremonies.

STEVENSON, MATILDA COXE
1904   *The Zuni Indians.* Bureau of American Ethnology, 23rd Annual Report, pp. 3-634.
        Profusely illustrated with many color plates of Zuni Kachina masks.

TITIEV, MISCHA

1944   *Old Oraibi.* Cambridge: Peabody Museum of American Archeology and
         Ethnology, vol. XXII, no. 1, 277 pp.
         Pp. 109-129 contains detailed description and analysis of the Kachina rites at
         Old Oraibi.

VOTH, H. R.

1901   *The Oraibi Powamu Ceremony.* Chicago: Field Columbian Museum,
         Anthropological Series, vol. 111, no. 2, 97 pp.
         A detailed description of the major ceremony of the Kachina cult, including the
         initiation of the young boys.

PLATES

PLATE I.

Soyal Kachina's costume is in keeping with his actions and gives a general appearance of great age. The cotton shirt and leggings are the old type formerly woven by the Hopi. He wears a white cotton blanket (cotton ceremonial fabrics are generally white-washed to make them whiter) and a skein of twisted black yarn across his right shoulder. The kilt, sash and belt are common to most Kachinas. The hands are painted white, with zig-zags wiped from the backs. Kachinas, with few exceptions, paint themselves so. Black yarn is tied to the right wrist and left leg. Below the right knee is a turtle shell rattle and in the right hand a gourd rattle. Hanging from the back of the belt is a fox skin. In the left hand is carried a sack of meal and four prayer sticks which are placed against the wall of the Winter Solstice kiva. Like most Chief Kachina masks, the one shown here is extremely plain. The tuft of dyed red horse hair on top of the mask has an eagle feather tied in it. An old fox skin forms the collar.

PLATE II.

Mastop Kachina's black and white mask has ears fashioned from corn husk and a collar of dried grass. A pair of black eagle feathers are tied to the top. The kilt is generally a dog skin but was formerly buffalo hide. The entire body is covered with black paint on which white hand prints appear. Two are in the middle of the back and sometimes on the back of the mask. Frog or lizard designs often replace the handprints on the mask. On the right hip is tied a rattle made from a mountain sheep horn and cow hooves. Mastop wears yarn on both wrists and legs and carries a sack of meal and a painted stick.

PLATE III.

Qöqölo Kachina is always dressed in old clothes. Formerly the costume was of buckskin, but the use of old suits and coats has been the rule for at least fifty years. The mask may be blue or yellow and the skins of several small birds are attached to it. Old sacking generally forms its base. This Kachina sings of game and good hunting and, after his own dance, will often become clownish and burlesque the dances of other societies. Manas similar to Hemis mana (Plate XV) sometimes accompany Qöqölo.

PLATE IV.

Eototo is the chief of all the Kachinas. The mask is made of buckskin or white cotton cloth and has sacred or magical properties. It is embellished with a few sparrow hawk feathers. The costume, except for the mask, is the same as worn by Soyal Kachina (Plate I). A bag of white cornmeal, a chief's stick, a netted gourd of water, and green corn shoots are carried. The chief's stick is shaped in a distinctive manner and has an ear of white corn tied to it.

PLATE V.

Aholi is Eototo's partner and follows him during the rites of the ninth day of Powamu ceremony. The conical mask has macaw feathers and red hair projecting from the top. A kilt, sash and belt are worn. The body, painted as Poli Kachina (Plate XXII), is partially covered by an antique robe which has a strange mythical figure of a man with the wings of a bird painted on the back. In the left hand objects similar to those of Eototo are carried and in the right, a staff.

PLATE VI.

Angwusnasomtaqa ("The one with crow tied on") is commonly referred to as the crow mother Kachina. She appears both in the children's initiation into the Kachina cult and in the morning ceremony on the last day of Powamu. When she comes in early morning, she is known as Angwushahai and at that time neither eyes nor mouth are indicated upon the face of the mask. The most striking feature is the crow wing tied to each side of the mask. On top are the soft white eagle feathers known as breath feathers to the Hopi. The collar is of spruce. She, like other female Kachinas. wears the belt tied at the left side—the large white wedding belt which is presented by every groom to his bride with her wedding costume. The robe is a bride's blanket, the borders embroidered in wool with familiar rain symbols. She wears a Hopi loomed dress and white buckskin moccasins. Her hands are painted white and she is carrying a plaque with corn and bean plants that have been grown in the kiva.

PLATE VII.

Hu' Kachina is the whipper who appears only when the children are initiated into the Kachina cult. His terrifying appearance can be attributed to the large mouth with bared teeth the projecting eyes and the horns from which eagle feathers dangle. A fan of eagle feathers projects backward from the mask top and a wildcat skin forms its base. The black horse hair beard has stripes of whitewash across it. He wears a breech cloth and a red horse hair kilt. The body is painted black and white. In each hand he carries yucca blades with which he administers the whipping. Two of these Kachinas perform at every initiation whipping.

PLATE VIII.

Hahai wuhti, a Kachina mother, is full of clownish good humor as she runs about jabbering in a high falsetto voice. The white mask has a downy eagle feather on top and a red bang between two small whorls of black hair. She wears dress, belt, moccasins and a red-and-black bordered maiden's blanket. In her right hand she holds a perfect ear of white corn while her left carries a gourd filled with water. In the course of her antics she often will pour water over the heads of her spectators. She is always found in the Pachavu procession and occasionally with other Kachina groups.

PLATE IX.

He'e'e is the warrior maiden Kachina. She is shown as she always appears, with her hair done up in a whorl on one side and hanging full length on the other. According to legend her mother was just putting up her hair when enemies came. She immediately jumped up, took her bow and quiver and rushed out to defend the village. She collects the Chief Kachinas for the Pachavu celebration and it is she who rushes to the housetops giving the signal for the Kachinas to drive all the spectators into their houses with whips. Over her shoulders she wears a blanket which is made of the same material as the loomed blanket dress. However, there is no red and green yarn striping as in the usual Hopi dress. Flowers of corn husk are attached.

PLATE X.

Soyok Wuhti is the leader of a group of monsters who make an annual round of the houses to punish all the disobedient children. The mask covers only the face. The beard is striped with white cornmeal or whitewash. Little rufts of cotton down adhere to her disheveled hair. In her left hand she carries a large knife or cleaver, often smeared with red to simulate blood. In her right she carries a crook with deer hooves tied to the upper end. She frequently uses this to reach out and catch children. Sometimes she carries a large basket on her back, into which is put food that is given to her. She wears a dress blanket as does He'e'e (Plate IX).

PLATE XI.

Na'tashka along with other fearful Kachinas accompanies the Soyok wuhti on her rounds. The long gourd snout is shown with terrifying teeth and cotton froth. Over his shoulders he wears a dyed sheepskin, a buckskin cape and a large turtle rattle below his knee. He whips his saw through the air and scrapes it down the house walls. The mouth opens and closes as he calls for children in a thick, rumbling voice. On the top of the mask is a cluster of owl feathers and on the back a spreading fan of eagle feathers tipped with breath feathers.

PLATE XII.

Tasapkachina (meaning Navaho Kachina) is one of the most popular of dancing Kachinas. The turquoise-colored mask has a yellow gourd beak. On the right side, red horse hair falls from a yellow knob out of which a white eagle feather projects. Across the top there is a bang of red hair and on the left, pheasant and eagle feathers surmount a cluster of owl feathers. The mask's top is covered with parrot and downy eagle feathers. The back is painted with cloud or rain symbols. The arm bands are woven from colored yarn. This Kachina wears a silver concha belt, and a wedding sash—sometimes called a rain belt—cascades to the ground.

PLATE XIII.

Tasapkachina mana (Navaho Kachina girl) accompanies Tasapkachina in day dances. Everything about this Kachina costume is typical of the Navaho woman's—the hair dress, velvet blouse, full billowing skirt, silver buttoned moccasins. She wears a silver concha belt and Navaho woven belt (red, green and white in contrast to the red, green and black of Hop belts).

PLATE XIV.

Hemis Kachina generally appears at Niman, the last masked dance of the year. The most unusual part of the mask is the cloud tablet superstructure, from the steps of which trimmed turkey feathers and long grasses project. Phallic symbols are painted on the front with a rainbow design in the center. The top is surmounted by two eagle tail feathers tipped with breath feathers. A cluster of eagle feathers is tied to the back of the mask and downy feathers float from many parts. The collar of the mask is made of spruce, and spruce is also inserted under the belt, in the arm bands and carried in the left hand. Spruce must be used by Kachinas performing the Niman and Powamu ceremonies, although other dancers may, if they wish, substitute cedar or juniper which is more easily procured. Hemis Kachina's body is painted black and a *paho* (prayer stick) is tied to his right wrist.

PLATE XV.

Hemis Kachina mana accompanies the Hemis Kachina. The hair is dressed in Hopi fashion. A downy eagle feather projects from the top of the yellow mask which is covered with a thin veil of red hair. At the base is a rainbow with a turquoise inlay at each end, below which is a fringe of small feathers. The belt, blanket and dress bordered with silver buttons are the same as previously noted. She carries a hollow gourd, notched stick and scapula (not shown) with which one of the basic rhythmical accompaniments of the song is produced.

PLATE XVII.

Hote, whose name is derived from his call, usually appears in mixed dances. This Kachina is a good example of the type with protruding eyes and may also appear in red or blue instead of the yellow mask shown. The mask has a split strand of yucca about the top and a downy feather dangles from the protruding snout. Small eagle feathers are thrust through the ears. Others, wrapped in cotton yarn, are fastened to the top of the mask. The most spectacular part of the costume is the eagle feather head dress similar to a warbonnet. Kachinas often carry roasted corn or other food which is given to the spectators after the dance.

PLATE XVIII.

Chöp Kachina (Deer Kachina) is very popular in mixed dances. The mask has a turquoise face and basketry visor from which are suspended small trimmed feathers. On either side are rosettes made of cottonwood, painted leather and red horsehair, and in back is a cluster of eagle feathers. The kilt is a red-and-black bordered maiden's blanket. A white belt, tied in the rear, supplants the more usual fox skin. The leggings are of buckskin and rain fringe is tied about the moccasins. This plate shows one of several variations in the costume of Chöp Kachina. However, the stick representing the forelegs is common to all variations as well as to other animal Kachinas.

PLATE XIX.

Ahote is extremely popular and his songs are well liked by the Hopi. The mask is distinguished by the horns. snout, bulbous eyes and painted design. A star is on the left side and a crescent moon on the right. Tied to the top is a bunch of parrot feathers and a fan-shaped spray of eagle feathers which projects backward. This black Ahote wears a buckskin kilt and paints his body black and yellow.

PLATE XX

Movitkuntaqa (The one who has a yucca kilt) is named from the most distinctive feature of his costume, a kilt fashioned from yucca leaves. Any bright cloth or shawl is used as an underskirt. The mask
is intricately adorned with paint, feathers and blossoms. A small bear paw appears below each eye.
This Kachina is carrying, besides bow and arrow, a gift of colored piki (native bread). He wears high
buckskin leggings and Hopi garters.

PLATE XXI.

Siyangephoya (left handed) is so named because he holds his gourd rattle in his left hand, has the turtle shell rattle under his left knee, and dances with his left foot. Before the dance begins, and between songs, these Kachinas trot about making amusing little bows to each other or to the spectators—as illustrated. The mask is black with a pad of brown sheepskin on top; on the back are painted frog, lizard or rain designs. A goatskin is tied at the left shoulder. The left half of the body is painted black, the right is striped black and white.

PLATE XXII

Poli Kachina (Butterfly Kachina), like Tasap mana (Plate XXIII), uses the face type mask. The hair falls over the left shoulder. The body is painted in a special design, red, yellow and blue, and the lively dance is performed barefooted. Bells and yarn are worn on both legs. The rattle is sometimes painted and he carries a flower made from colored yarns. On his back is worn an elaborate tablet with eagle feathers at the top and bottom and a fringe of red horse hair at the sides. Poli Kachina and his partner (Plate XIII) always appear together and only in night dances. They, unlike most Kachinas, follow a dance pattern which involves much posturing of the body, and they are not strictly line dancers since they change positions inside the kiva. Most of the steps and dance forms are similar to the unmasked social Butterfly dance.

PLATE XXIII.

Poli Kachina mana (Butterfly Kachina girl) is the partner for Poli Kachina (Plate XXII). She wears an elaborate mask with towering headdress of varying design, from the base of which inlaid turquoise pendants hang. Poli Kachina mana carries evergreen in each hand and wears a bright shawl and anklets. These dancers—rarely more than four pairs—are accompanied by a masked chorus and drummer.

PLATE XXIV

Navan Kachina is a modern or new Kachina, although the only specific innovation is the velvet tunic with ribbons attached to it. He is a typical example of what is known as "fine clothes" Kachinas, who are often extremely gaudy. Clustered at the back of the mask are eagle feathers and on top, downy feathers and artificial flowers. White rabbit wool is wound about the base of the snout, and turquoise bobs are inserted in the ears.

PLATE XXV.

Qa'ö Kachina (Corn Kachina) dances with such a lively tempo that generally only boys or young men take this part. Like the Poli dancers, but unlike most Kachinas, they do not sing, but are accompanied by a drummer and masked chorus, generally of Koyemsi (mud heads). Both the dance and the songs have a certain gaiety and charm unusual to Kachinas. Qa'ö masks are decorated in a variety of geometric patterns. The top is covered with colored yarn from which four large turkey feathers project and between which are draped colored ribbons. The body is painted with blue circles, and red-and-green skeins of yarn are tied about the wrists and legs. Hopi belt, breech cloth, socks, garters, bells and moccasins complete the costume.

PLATE XXVI.

Huhuwa Kachina is known as the Crossed Legged One, for he walks and dances with his legs crossed. The costume varies considerably, but generally consists of dilapidated clothing and burlap sacks tied on the feet for moccasins. Ribbons are attached to the shirt and an abalone shell hangs from his neck. Huhuwa is said to be a very old Kachina and his mask is quite human in appearance, there being a wide variety in facial caricature. Three colored corn husk flowers decorate his woolly hair.

PLATE XXVII.

Kwikwilyaqa is the imitating Kachina. His distinguishing trait is manifested at the Pachavu ceremony when many different Kachinas swarm through the village, and at dances where he acts as a foil for the clowns. He echoes every spoken word seemingly regardless of language, and mimics with mirror-like rapidity every action and gesture of the person before him. Kwikwilyaqa wears a tousled cedar bark wig. His conical eyes and snout are decorated with black and white rings. The rest of the costume is optional.

PLATE XXVIII.

Talmopiya'akya is a Kachina acquired from Zuni. At First Mesa he is called by the Zuni name—Shipikne. Like the Corn Kachina he does not sing, but is exceptional because he uses no bells or rattles and the complete silence of his rapid dance inspires considerable awe. A pair of Talmopiya'akya often come with mixed groups. The one illustrated is painted black and represents the nadir; his companion is painted in many colors to represent the zenith. They carry yucca whips which are put into instant action, if spectators venture too close. The collar is of crow or raven feathers and the carved bird atop the mask has pheasant tail feathers. The kilt is embroidered cotton and the body is painted yellow and black, like Angakchina (Plate XVI). Two thongs are worn over the shoulders with tiny white shells attached. Talmopiya'akya dances barefoot with anklets of evergreen.